# TOMATO TALK

THE GIRL IN THE GARDEN

Tina Reich

Tina Reich
Turlock, California

Copyright © 2022 by Tina Reich.

All rights reserved. No part of this publication may be reproduced, distributed or transmitted in any form or by any means, including photocopying, recording, or other electronic or mechanical methods, without the prior written permission of the publisher, except in the case of brief quotations embodied in critical reviews and certain other noncommercial uses permitted by copyright law. For permission requests, write to the publisher, addressed "Attention: Permissions Coordinator," at the address below.

Tina Reich
Thegirlinthegarden77@gmail.com

Ordering Information:
Quantity sales. Special discounts are available on quantity purchases by corporations, associations, and others. For details, contact the "Special Sales Department" at the email address above.

Tomato Talk/ Tina Reich —1st ed.
ISBN 978-1-7343186-1-6

Dedication

To Kyle Reich; My son, my best friend, my advisor and always my biggest supporter.

With much love, I dedicate this book to you.

Disclaimer

This book is written to provide inspiration to those who want to start a vegetable garden.

The information provided is my opinion based on Google searches, books, YouTube Channels, and my own experiments.

This book is not meant to be a substitute for doing your own research.

I am not an expert in gardening, nor am I a trained chef.

Although I am not a comedian, I inserted my brand of humor.

# Introduction

Welcome to Tomato Talk!

I began gardening around 2019. The more I gardened, the more vegetables I harvested. Then I needed to eat or use them before they were rotten or process them for long-term storage.

That's when and why my research into YouTube, books and Google started. I found I was going to multiple places to get the information to plant, grow, harvest, and then process the 'fruits' of my labor.

Let's see. What are my choices? I could freeze them or dehydrate them. I could use them fresh from the garden. I could pressure-can my veggies.

Once a decision has been made on how to process them, what recipes do I have to use them in?

I have taken lots of notes in several notebooks, most of which I've put up where my Alaskan Malamute, Atka, can't get to them. This also means I've forgotten where I've put them.

I've gathered the notebooks I could find and I'm putting all my gathered information in one place

I'm starting this process with tomatoes.

Let's get started on our tomato journey.

The Great Debate!

Are tomatoes a fruit or vegetable?

After reading several definitions and watching multiple YouTube channels, what I understand is a fruit is the part of the plant/tree we eat that contains seeds. This means technically tomatoes are fruit.

But once, long, long ago, to be more specific in the 19th century, the Port Authority of New York classified tomatoes as a vegetable and therefore they were subject to the 10% import tax.

There was a tomato importer that did not want to pay the tax on imported vegetables, so he took it to the supreme court to prove the tomato was in fact a fruit.

The supreme court's decision was that tomatoes are a vegetable because they are served with a meal such as dinner and not served as a dessert.

Now I'm pretty sure that we can find dessert recipes with tomatoes. But on with the story.

The poor tomato importer was still stuck with the 10% tax.

You can read this information in much more detail at:

https://www.npr.org/sections/money/2013/12/26/256586055/when-the-supreme-court-decided-tomatoes-were-vegetables

One popular dude, that tomato!

Home gardening is on the rise and over 80% of folks that have a home garden grow tomatoes.

They are so easy to grow, or so it seems. You just put them in the garden where they will get lots of sunshine and you water them. Drum roll please ……. now you have home grown tomatoes.

Well, if it's that easy, let's try it!

It may be socially unacceptable for us to talk to ourselves in some circles, but in the gardening circle it's perfectly fine to ask ourselves these questions.

Will we be starting our tomatoes with seeds, or will we buy plants at the local nursery?

Do we want determinate or indeterminate tomatoes?

Determinate will set all their fruit at once. Indeterminate tomatoes continue to set fruit throughout the growing season. If we are unsure about the tomato variety that we've picked, we can always google it.

Heirloom vs hybrid... I'm still learning about this topic. But if I am understanding correctly, if we want to save seeds from this year's crop, we should buy heirloom.

Let me give you the YouTube channel I watched when I was researching these topics.

https://www.youtube.com/c/EpicGardening

Now that we have thoroughly talked to ourselves, let's gather our supplies and get down to planting.

If you purchased tomatoes from your local nursery, skip down to transplanting.

We need something to start seeds in such as an egg carton, old nursery 4 packs, even red solo cups. Whatever you are using, be sure there are holes in the bottom for watering and drainage. The exception to that is if you are using an egg carton. It will soak up water quickly and dry quickly so keep an eye on this kind of container.

We need soil. They have soil specific for seed starting, but I usually use whatever soil I have on hand.

Next, we fill our container with soil and water thoroughly, not soggy and dripping with water, but nice and damp.

We need to read our packet of seeds. It will give you lots of information, including how deep to plant that specific seed.

Once we've got our seeds planted and assuming we will plant a variety of seeds, we need to label them.

I have tried several ways to label my seeds, and none worked very well. My suggestion is to buy the plastic nursery garden stakes. On Amazon they are about $5 for 100.

Now we need to keep our seeds moist and warm until they germinate.

Here is a link to my video where I talk about doing all of this on a budget:

https://youtu.be/CoNE7yecpG8


Don't leaf me now.

When our seeds germinate, they will have two leaves, these are their 'first leaves'.

Soon more leaves will appear looking more like tomato leaves and these are the true leaves.

Depending on what we've planted our seeds in, we may need to transplant into a bigger container while they continue grow and get big enough to transplant.

When our plants are several inches tall, and we are just a week or two away from wanting to put them in the garden, we need to harden them off. In other words, get them used to the outside weather.

I take mine out and put them some place where they have shade but eventually will get some direct sunlight. It's important you check your soil and do not let your seedlings dry out.

After a week or two, it's time to transplant our seedlings.

Are you feeling cagey?

Yes! Today is transplant day. Let's get our soil damp and dig our little holes. We want our holes deep enough that we plant 2/3 of our seedling in the soil.

We need to put a tomato cage around our little plants to keep them upright while they grow. This will encourage our tomato plants to grow up towards the sky. It will give support to the branches and keep our tomatoes off the ground.

Continue to water and watch it grow!

The toxic tomato? Is it fact or fiction?

The story goes something like this. The European aristocrats would get sick and die after consuming tomatoes. Why? Tomatoes are high in acidity so when the wealthy Europeans served them on their pewter plates the acidity of the tomato would leach the lead out of the plate thus causing death. During this time nothing was known about lead poisoning, so the tomato took the rap.

I was surprised to find a couple of YouTube videos that also talk about this story. Here are the links so you can hear more of the story.

https://www.youtube.com/watch?v=AG9Oc6TxDXU

https://www.youtube.com/watch?v=beBQgxdu2eY&t=316s

Is that Wally the worm or Charlie the caterpillar?

I encountered my first tomato hornworm this growing season. He was absolutely ginormous! Does that mean he'd been there for years?

No, thank goodness but once they hatch they are full grown in 3-4 weeks.

These very ugly pests will devour your tomato plants so look often. I have heard they will illuminate under a black light, so my black light flashlight is on order.

I put on my gloves and picked off this devil looking creature and chopped him in half.

There are many pests and diseases that can attack your plant so while you wait to harvest don't forget to give them a good 'once over' when you water.

If you smoke, (quit now!) do NOT smoke in your garden or touch your plants soon after you've touched a cigarette. There is a percentage of tobacco that may be infected with a virus that can infect and attack your tomatoes. Keep all tobacco products out of your garden.

Be sure to plant flowers and herbs to attract the beneficial creatures like lady bugs, butterflies, praying mantis and bees.

Stay organic. Use sprays only when you have a pest problem and sprays that will NOT harm the beneficial creatures.

Happy Harvesting!

It's finally time! Time to harvest our home-grown tomatoes. Or so we thought.

You get out to the garden and wow there are only 4 tomatoes to harvest. The rest are still green.

Well get those 4 harvested and get to the kitchen.

How are we going to process them?

We can eat them freshly sliced.

We can make fresh salsa.

We can dehydrate and make tomato powder.

We can wash and dry them and place them in the freezer until we have a big enough harvest to make a batch of…….well, of whatever we decide when we get there.

Once a tomato has been frozen the texture will change when it thaws. It will not have the same texture as fresh from the garden or store. They will be great for sauces and such but not for slicing.

I am one of those cooks that say a pinch of that and dash of this. Keep that in mind as you are reading my recipe, or should I say experiment, for home-made tomato sauce.

I have put 3-4 tomatoes in my freezer each day, for several days. I finally have enough to make tomato sauce. I take them out of the freezer the day before and let them thaw in the refrigerator.

Tomato Sauce experiment

We love our tomato sauce. I have not yet experimented making this on the stove top or slow cooker.

Instant Pot
immersion blender

4 tablespoons of olive oil
3 medium red onions; I slice into rings
2 large carrots; I use these to sweeten the sauce without having to add sugar. Roughly chop
1 celery stalk; optional and only do this is I have celery on hand. Roughly chop
6 pounds of tomatoes; I have used Roma tomatoes most often, but I do use whatever I grow. I quarter the tomatoes

When I have had a stray bell pepper or zucchini left from the garden, I chop them up and throw them in the pot. When I do this I usually add 1 more carrot.

In the instant pot Sauté the veggies for 5-6 minutes and then add the tomatoes. Mash the tomatoes down so the juices can begin to flow.

When this all begins to bubble switch to pressure cooker and cook for 5 minutes. Let the steam release naturally when it's done.

Put your instant pot on a sauté or soup setting and simmer for another hour. Be sure to stir frequently.

Once the cooking is done take an immersion blender and blend away to ensure there are no chunks.

This sauce will be VERY HOT!!! Wear gloves or let it cool a little before blending. If you are going to use your regular blender the sauce will need to cool down for some time before blending.

Let the sauce completely cool. You can then freeze in ice trays. I recommend measuring how much fits in the ice tray. This way you know how much to thaw for dinner. Or you can measure out a specific amount and put it in a labeled zip lock bag and freeze laying the bags flat.

You may find that you must use a little more seasoning when you are creating your favorite sauces. Here are a few ideas that start with tomato sauce: Marinara sauce, Pizza sauce, Spaghetti sauce, Chili, Tomato soup.

This is NOT an approved recipe for canning. Please be sure to use the USDAs recommendations when canning or dehydrating any foods.

**National Center for home food preservation**
https://nchfp.uga.edu/#gsc.tab=0

**USDA Home Canning methods**
https://www.nifa.usda.gov/about-nifa/blogs/usdas-complete-guide-home-canning

If you've had a large tomato harvest and you've used the recipe above to make home-made tomato sauce, then you also know it does take up space in your freezer.

Yes! I noticed that as well.

I did some research and guess what I learned?! You can dehydrate tomatoes. So, let's step into the world of dehydrating tomatoes for a moment or two.

Dehydrating tomatoes can be done in the oven as well as a dehydrator. I use a dehydrator.

To experiment I took 4 tomatoes and washed them well. I dried them off and then cut them into slices. The slices were about ¼ inch thick. I spread them on my dehydrator trays and turned them on dehydrate at 120 degrees and 20 hours. I started checking them about 8 hours. Some got nice and crispy by 10 and others took longer. If they snapped between my fingers, I knew they were good and dry.

Funny fact; I do not like tomatoes. They are slimy. But I like multiple tomato products. So, I thought hmmmm lets taste a dehydrated tomato. I liked it! No slime! A tomato chip is a lot healthier than a potato chip (store bought of course). Also, it has a very intense tomato flavor.

Let's watch me taste a dehydrated tomato!
https://youtu.be/Y4NfjdDXR1M


Now that I have tomato chips what do I do with them?

Let's make tomato powder! Why? Because, if I remember correctly dehydrated food retains 85% of its nutrients. This means I can get the benefits of eating tomatoes by adding tomato powder to my food.  Or that is what I'm thinking. I'm no expert so please do not quote me and do your own research.

Take your tomato chips and use a blender, food processor, or my favorite a coffee been grinder and grind them up until they become a smooth powder.
And now you're asking what am I going to do with tomato powder?  Well let's experiment.

Experiment 1
Tomato Juice

Experiment 2
Sauce

Experiment 3
Paste


I bet your wondering why there is no information under these first 3 experiments.  That is because I did find a YouTube channel and she has recipe amounts for these and more.  So instead of doing my own experiments I'm going to first start with her measurements and adjust to my liking as I go.  Here is the link to her YouTube channel.

https://www.youtube.com/c/PrepperPotpourri/videos

https://www.youtube.com/watch?v=kswk2Y0_OE&t=113s

Experiment 4

Scrambled Eggs

My first experiment I only used ¼ teaspoon of tomato powder and I could not taste tomato. I updated my experiment so that next time I remember to add ½ teaspoon. I will continue to increase how much tomato powder I use based on the flavor and what I like. I'm just happy I am now getting all the nutrients a tomato has to offer.

2 eggs
½ teaspoon tomato powder
Salt, pepper, or any other seasonings you like
Whisk together well and scramble up some eggs!

Your experiment:

_____

_____

## Experiment 5

### Tomato basil spread/dip

When I tried this experiment the first thing I did was add the tomato powder to the sour cream and put it in the refrigerator overnight. I wanted my tomato powder to reconstitute to a point where it would not be gritty.

The next day I used my hand-held blender and blended in the cream cheese and other spices. But it just didn't have much flavor. I added more seasonings and that's when I decided to try ¼ teaspoon of cayenne pepper in it. I whipped it again. I gave it a taste and just like I thought the new tomato powder I had added was gritty. But the cayenne gave it a nice bite. I placed it back in the fridge overnight.

I am very excited to say I love this experiment. However, I will reduce the amount of cayenne or leave it out altogether. Below is the experiment I'll use from now on.

8 oz sour cream
4 oz cream cheese
4 tablespoons tomato powder
1 tablespoon basil
1 teaspoon salt
1 teaspoon garlic powder
1/8 teaspoon cayenne pepper (optional)

Your experiment:

_____

_____

Experiment 6

Taco meatloaf

I had three taste testers besides myself. I liked it but thought that the bean topping was lacking in flavor. My son ate a slice and went back for seconds. My friend Lorna felt the same as me, the bean topping was lacking in flavor. Her husband thought it was creative and delish.

The green chilis I used are poblanos and Jalapeños from last year's garden. I tossed them in the freezer last year, now I take out what I need for a recipe and chop them before they thaw.

The breadcrumbs are homemade with no seasonings. Leftover bread I dehydrated and ran through my grinder.

The eggs are from my backyard chickens, so they are about the medium size you'd buy at the store.

1 lb ground beef
1 lb ground pork
½ cup breadcrumbs
½ cup diced green chilis
Medium onion
I Taco seasoning packet
2 tablespoons tomato powder
½ cup shredded Mexican blend cheese
2 eggs

I mixed all the ingredients together. I placed in equal amounts of the mix in 4 small loaf pans. I baked on 350F for 30 minutes. When I removed from the oven to add the bean topping, I poured out any grease that had accumulated.

1 can refried Beans (I used spicy jalapeño)
½ teaspoon tomato powder
I warmed the refried beans and added ½ teaspoon of tomato powder until well combined. I spread the beans on top of the meat loaf, and I topped with shredded cheddar cheese and baked until cheese was melted, about 10 minutes.

Your experiment:

_____
_____

Experiment 7

Taco meatloaf

Yes, I tried one more time. You'll see the changes below. The flavors just didn't work together. I'm not sure if it's because I only had chili lime refried beans or if it was the green enchilada sauce. This specific experiment is a FAIL. Or it is the beginning of a WIN! Don't be afraid to experiment.

The green chilis I used are poblanos and Jalapeños from last year's garden. I tossed them in the freezer last year, now I take out what I need for a recipe and chop them before they thaw.

The breadcrumbs are a hot and spicy variety from the store. It was all I had.

The eggs are from my backyard chickens, so they are about the medium size you'd buy at the store.


1 lb ground beef
1 lb ground pork
½ cup breadcrumbs
½ cup diced green chilis
Medium onion
I Taco seasoning packet
2 tablespoons tomato powder
½ cup shredded Mexican blend cheese
2 eggs

First, I mixed the egg, tomato powder and taco seasoning. I let it set for just a couple of minutes for the powders to soak in some moisture. I whipped the egg mixture again until it looked like all the seasonings were incorporated well.

Then I added the egg mixture to the ground beef and pork and mixed well. I put it in the refrigerator for a couple of hours. I thought it was going to be a couple of hours, but I actually didn't get back to this experiment until the next day.

I added the onions, green peppers, breadcrumbs and cheese.

I mixed altogether. I placed in 5 small loaf pans. I baked on 350F for 30 minutes. I took each loaf and poured out the grease that had accumulated.

1 can refried Beans (All I had was chili lime)
½ teaspoon tomato powder
½ cup shredded Mexican blend cheese
1/3 cup green enchilada sauce


I poured about 2 tablespoons of green sauce over the meatloaf. I warmed the refried beans and 1/3 cup of the green sauce until well combined. Then added ½ teaspoon of tomato powder, mixing well. I spread that over the meatloaf, I topped with shredded cheddar cheese and baked until cheese was melted, about 10 minutes.

Your experiment:

_____

_____

These are just experiments. Something I thought would be fun to do. But we don't really need to reinvent the wheel. We all have our grandmother's meatloaf recipe so add your tomato powder to the recipe.

How many ideas can we come up with to use tomato powder and help our meals have more nutrients?

Stew
Chili
Soup
Tacos
Sprinkled or mixed in with a salad dressing
Mashed potatoes
Homemade focaccia bread
Mixed with butter and garlic for garlic bread
Mixed in mayonnaise to use on sandwiches or burgers for people who don't like tomato texture
Scrambled eggs
Quiche

Your ideas

_____
_____

Here are a few of the resources I use.

National Center for home food preservation
https://nchfp.uga.edu/#gsc.tab=0
Please be safe in all ways that you process and store your food. Always do the research!

USDA Home Canning methods
https://www.youtube.com/watch?v=Xn69q6eeGM0
I did not talk about canning for a few reasons. The biggest reason is I have not done any canning yet.

RoseRed Homestead
https://www.youtube.com/c/RoseRedHomestead/videos

The Purposeful Pantry
https://www.youtube.com/c/ThePurposefulPantry

Mary's Nest
https://www.youtube.com/c/MarysNest/videos

Tasting History with Max Miller
https://www.youtube.com/c/MarysNest/videos

EPIC Gardening
https://www.youtube.com/c/EpicGardening/videos

Prepper Potpourri
https://www.youtube.com/c/PrepperPotpourri/videos

Acknowledgements

I have many people to thank for helping and supporting my efforts on writing my first tiny book.

My taste testers Lorna and Jay Cook, Kyle Reich, and Scott Wagner.
Hey you're still alive!

For reading and providing feedback Lisa Mangino, Ruth Kaber, Kari Heath, and Joseph King.
How many times did you fall asleep?

Kim Novak and Lorna Cook for looking at my layout and giving some wonderful ideas that I think make this book great.

The entire team at Get It Done Tiny Book course.
A great team!

I'm sure I'm forgetting several people.  A big thank you to everyone!
.

About the Author

I was born and raised in the Central Valley in California. I live with my son, 3 dogs and 2 chickens.

I have written three children's books that you can find on Amazon:
https://www.amazon.com/s?k=Tina+Reich&crid=1YCDH1IVFWUFE&sprefix=tina+reich%2Caps%2C206&ref=nb_sb_noss

Be Happy with What You Have
How Popo Got his name
Ella's Big Catch

I have a blog which you can find at: https://teawithtina.net

You can find my YouTube channel at:
https://www.youtube.com/channel/UC8FhnKmBd7rA5tuRmBFdUUQ

www.ingramcontent.com/pod-product-compliance
Lightning Source LLC
Chambersburg PA
CBHW071918070526
44583CB00016B/2046